#100

Best Life Lessons

You'll Wish

You knew

Before college,

and

The real world

On starting on your best foot today.

For the young soul at heart who is ready

to take a chance on their dream

and make it happen!

You'll wish someone had told you this before
growing up.

Preface

While I'm sure there are many great advices out there for you, I thought I'd sum up a few that made a big positive impact in my life. I hope they do the same for you.

Dedicated to you

May this book open up

a new world for you,

and bring you joy for

your entire existence.

Table of Contents

This is your life, make it count…

"What you think

you become.

What you feel

you attract.

What you imagine

 you create."

Buddha

This is your life, make it count…

Find three hobbies you love:

One to make you Money,

one to keep you in Shape,

and one to be Creative.

This is your life, make it count…

"When nobody else celebrates you, learn to celebrate yourself. When nobody else compliments you, then compliment yourself. It's not up to other people to keep you encouraged. It's up to you. Encouragement should come from the inside."

-Joel Osteen

This is your life, make it count...

Your mind is your instrument; learn to be its master and not its slave.

This is your life, make it count…

"Surround yourself only with people who are going to take you higher"

-Oprah Winfrey

This is your life, make it count…

"Success is doing what you want, when you want, where you want, with whom you want, as much as you want."

-Anthony Robbins

Define what success means to you. Some people have chased the corporate life and have achieved great success, but still found themselves unhappy. Finding out what truly matters to you will not only save you time in accomplishing success, but it will make the path that you need to take toward it just a tad bit clearer.

This is your life, make it count…

Live less out of habit, and more out of intent.

This is your life, make it count…

Find the feeling place of your new desire, if you wish to bring it into your reality.

When you feel the way it is to have what it is that you want, it will come to you much quicker. For example when people say they want to have lots of money, they may simply be wishing for the comfort that money can provide, Like having the freedom to do nothing today if they so wish, or having the freedom to fly off somewhere with their whole family.

Most people usually just want freedom of time. Get specific with the universe.

This is your life, make it count…

Start a big vision board early on, because everything you place on it comes to you. Yes it's like scrapbooking, except you're creating your life instead.

This is your life, make it count...

"Choose your expectations practice it, make it your own, and your universe will bring it to you."

-Abraham Hicks

College life and decisions…

Go to college because you want to, not because you have been fed the lie that it will give a great job in return.

I believe that life is all about learning and when we stop learning, we stop living.

There are so many ways a person can make it nowadays with the world becoming so internet savvy and all. If you're good at something you can focus on mastering yourself on that topic without the propaganda of college; paying such an outrageous amount of money to take classes you don't even really need for the sake of the school institutions' pocket is just ridiculous.

College life and decisions…

Meditate before you start your day!
Meditate before you do anything. In order to get
the outcome you want in a situation. You must
see it in your mind, in the utmost positive
conclusion.

Meditate before your first school day, your
exams, before graduation (so you don't trip on
stage lol), your interviews, your awesome trip
across the world, or whatever it happens to be
for you.

We are creators, and we are creating every
second in every day. Better it be for something
we want, rather than something we don't.

College life and decisions…

"Whatever you want your job to be, make sure it's something you enjoy doing"

Ever hear the saying "Follow your Passion"? Well, you probably should because that's the only way you'll be able to go on once you get in the real world, and are no longer in the comfort of your parents' home.

At least if you have a job that allows you to do exactly what you like to do, you won't feel the need to complain or escape from it. You'll feel at home.

College Life and Decisions…

"The greatest gift you can give to someone is giving them the greatest expectations of themselves."

Abraham Hicks

College Life and Decisions…

"There is nothing noble in being superior to your fellow man; true nobility is being superior to your former self."

Ernest Hemingway

College Life and Decisions…

401 k is an important investment decision for your future and the beautiful family you may plan on having.

Yes you may still party, but still invest in your future. Your kids, significant other or pets will thank you for it.

College Life and Decisions…

Get a job, or career that offers great benefits.

We don't really think about these things when we're young because somehow we think we're invincible; but it's truly important. You never know when you might need a physical, an MRI, or be lifted up on a helicopter (knock on wood) from one of your adventurous vacations.

College Life and Decisions…

Keep your arts or doodles, they might be worth something later, it could be turned into a best-selling art book or something. Who knows? The world is full of surprises.

I mean seriously! Have you seen Kim Kardashian's new purse of her daughter's drawings? What about Angelina Jolie's wedding dress to Brad? It's full of her children's arts and doodles? Just pure genius, I daresay!

College Life and Decisions…

Keep your four line poems, they're not gibberish thoughts. There's actually a college major out there that it falls into. It's called, creative writing.

College Life and Decisions…

If you want a pet, get one.

The love of a pet is incomparable. They love so genuinely that your heart will grow an inch every time you cuddle them. They can sense your emotions and will console you if you need a pick me up.

College Life and Decisions…

Same goes for a parent. If your child loves animals, let them get one, at least.

Yes they should take care of it. It will teach them responsibility and it will allow them to care for someone other than themselves. There are no words to describe the bond.

College Life and Decisions...

You should purposely create your life every day. This is why you were born with the power to do so. Don't make the mistake of living life in Autopilot. Things don't just happen to you. You ask for them, therefore they come to you.

College Life and Decisions…

"Take chances, make mistakes, and get messy!"

- Ms. Frizzle

College Life and Decisions…

"Follow your intuition.

Be smart,

Be brave,

Tell the truth.

& don't take any shit from anyone."

-Kelly Cutrone

College Life and Decisions…

Train yourself to find the blessing in everything.

College Life and Decisions…

"When in doubt, take a nap!"

J. Kelly

Taking a break from the problem may be just what you need. If you find that you cannot come up with the solution you want, taking a break to ponder or to do something else to distract yourself may very well solve the problem for you.

College Life and Decisions…

"Be brave, take risks. Nothing can substitute life experiences."

-Paulo Coelho

College Life and Decisions…

"True humility is staying teachable, regardless of how much you already know."

-CG

College Life and Decisions…

Thank the heavens every day for your life, your health, your family, your friends and your wealth.

College Life and Decisions…

"Be in love with your life. Every minute of it."

-Jack Kerouac

College Life and Decisions…

"Every day you have to reinvent yourself."

-Oscar de la Renta

College Life and Decisions…

You will only be this version of yourself in this lifetime, might as well make it amusing.

College Life and Decisions…

See the Beauty in everything around you.

College Life and Decisions…

Follow your "I am's" with something wonderful.

College life and decisions…

Fall in love, but fix the tunnel vision.

He's not the only guy or girl in the world you know! You should make time for your friends and family and all your other activities too so that you're not left disoriented if the relationship doesn't work out. That crazy sensation you feel when you're around your crush, or the feeling that they're the most beautiful creature that could ever grace this planet. Believe me looking back it will seem just a tad bit ridiculous, but you'll get to smile to yourself, so I guess it's not all bad.

College life and decisions…

Go easy on the loans!

If you have to get them, really evaluate how much you'll be able to pay monthly after you graduate. Get a part-time job to pay for at least half of the tuition bill. Your budget will thank you later when the interests start capitalizing and you hate school and there's no way you're going back to freeze them. LOL

College life and decisions…

Intern more.

The college books only take you so far. You have to get out there to receive the hands-on learning you'll need in the real world, and create the contacts you'll need to start your career on the right foot after graduation.

College life and decisions…

Don't get a brand new car right out of college.

Especially if you took loans out (unless you had a chunk of the money saved already). Just think how handy the extra $300-400 can be for you. Not only that, being right out of college are usually full of unknown stages where anything can happen, with having to start a career and making sure it's the path you want to be in; and if it's not to have the courage to switch.

That's too much uncertainty to have in your life at that point; to go add a car note on top of your other bills would be a mistake.

College life and decisions…

Hey you don't want to work for somebody else?

Or your job just doesn't exist yet? Create it! Sometimes you just have to create your own opportunity.

College life and decisions…

If you're not having fun, you're doing it wrong.

In life you have to always do what is important to you no matter who disagrees or don't understand.

College life and decisions…

We are all growing up, we will be trying different things, and starting businesses; we have to support each other.

Network while you're in college, make new friends and stay in contact. Those are the people who may end up being on the same path of success as you.

College life and decisions…

What they don't tell you about the interview scene after graduation is that it sucks!

You go through a bunch of interviews trying to convince random people to hire you for a possible job you won't even like two-weeks or a month later. Talk about waste of time and talent.

This is why finding your niche is truly important, or you'll spend your precious innovative time doing work that doesn't inspire your soul and only drains you.

College life and decisions…

Anticipate success!

It's another form of visualizing; be in the moment every time, be present!

College life and decisions…

"Make sure the gift you want to share with the world is an honest expression of what's in your heart."

-Russell Simmons

College life and decisions…

"Accepting that you don't need things to be happy is exactly how you can develop the Faith and Courage to get the things you desire."

-Russell Simmons

College life and decisions…

If you do go to college make sure it's for something that you have a true interest in. Otherwise your grades will suffer and therefore your perfect GPA.

College life and decisions…

You'll need to develop some serious life balance between work and school.

And if you're serious about your degree, it must always come first, no matter what your supervisor say. Repeating the year is never fun; you can always look for a different job but you can't get a wasted year of school back.

Reach for more…

"What you seek is seeking you."

-Rumi

Reach for more…

Create something new today, even if it's doodling on a piece of paper or writing the next Harry Potter. Just keep creating.

Reach for more…

Life is about rediscovering yourself every day.

Reach for more…

Give yourself the chance to reach your full potential.

Reach for more…

Explore your interest more and do more of what makes you happy; that's the true meaning of life.

Find out more of what you like to do, make it an adventure and remember to have fun. The best relationship you will ever have is with yourself.

Reach for more…

More fun equals more blessings, which equals more fun, which equals more blessings. It's the circle of life.

Reach for more…

Never give up on yourself or this life because you'll come back and find yourself in the same situation; some of which are called Deja vu. There's a lesson to be learned in every situation.

Reach for more…

Start creating your own legacy today.

Reach for more…

Start spreading your good karma out in the world today. You never know when you might need some to rescue you.

Reach for more…

Allow the intelligent being that is your soul to express itself through you.

Reach for more…

Creation is intelligence having fun.

Reach for more…

Life is about giving and expressing yourself, whether it's through your work or actions. Find or do something that brings meaning to your life.

Reach for more…

"Create a sanctuary for your soul."

Somewhere you can go to breathe, to meditate, paint, or to do whatever it is that brings you peace.

Reach for more…

The most beautiful thing in the world you can be is yourself!

No one can experience this life through your eyes, and your soul in the same way that you can. So get out there and create as much as you can, and go on as many adventures as you want to.

Reach for more…

Create a goal list, accomplish them, create a new list, and repeat!

Reach for more…

Until you discover your worth, you will never see what God truly has in mind for you.

Reach for more…

Follow your Bliss!

I always loved that expression. Doing more of what you love to do will undoubtedly bring you better things to love and appreciate.

Reach for more…

Take that art class! Explore your creative side.

Create a masterpiece or create something ridiculously childish that you can't help but laugh at every time you look at it. Either way you'll win.

Reach for more…

"Vision is the art of seeing what is invisible to others."

-Jonathan Swift

Reach for more…

"No person is free he who is not master of himself."

-Epictetus

Reach for more…

Do more of what makes you happy.

For example, I'm guilty of putting my Christmas tree up way in the middle of November, simply for the fact that I love the lights so much. Something about a fully decorated tree just brightens my day every time I look at it.

Circle of Life…

Whenever something happens that makes you sad, ask yourself whether you'd still care about it when you're ninety.

Circle of Life…

"A wise man, recognizing that the world is but an illusion, does not act as if it is real, so (therefore) he escapes the suffering."

Gautama   Buddha

Circle of Life…

"When we activate something without resistance, it comes fast!"

Abraham Hicks

Circle of Life…

In life you must make time for both your love one and your passion; one nourishes the heart, the other, the soul.

Circle of Life...

Feed your mind. Do the things that brings you joy, things that only you like. Your soul will thank you for it.

Circle of Life…

Everything you need is already within.

Circle of Life…

"Always laugh when you can, it is cheap medicine."

-Lord Byron

Circle of Life…

Create a specific place in your home, a place where no negative thoughts can enter. Your soul needs it, like a plant needs water to bloom.

Circle of Life…

"Imagination is the preview to life's upcoming attractions."

-Albert Einstein

Circle of Life…

"What is the point of being alive if you don't at least try to do something remarkable?"

-John Green

Circle of Life…

Your value doesn't decrease based on someone's inability to see your worth.

Circle of Life…

Tell your story; that story that's suffocating you; tell it good and then close that chapter of your life for good.

Try not to dwell on your negative past, it will only mess up your chances in the present and will keep repeating itself.

Circle of Life…

Be strong enough to let go and wise enough to accept what you want!

Circle of Life…

Courage is doing something despite being fearful.

Circle of Life…

Spend on experiences, not things.

How you feel when you think about the memories from the experiences tend to last longer than the impulsive decision to buy that purse, or 50inch TV.

Circle of Life…

Spend more time with family.

Don't let your present or future hectic schedule get in the way. They're an important part of your journey too.

Circle of Life…

Travel as much as you can, for it's in doing so that you'll see the world's true beauty.

Circle of Life…

Travel alone.

Meet new people and form new lifetime friendship. There's a true sense of independency that you feel when you're out on your own.

Circle of Life...

Travel with Friends.

Ok this one you can still do later on, but it can get sort of hectic trying to get everyone's schedule to align; so the earlier the better, with no job schedules, and no babies to worry about.

Circle of Life…

Eat healthy, and see yourself in a healthy body.

Some people focus too much on their body or weight problems; that's the reason it never improves. If you really can't find positive things to say about your body, distract yourself with something fun, while you retrain your mind.

Circle of Life…

Decide on your life goals, write them down on paper.

Place it on that vision board that we talked about earlier.

Circle of Life…

Live the life of your dreams.

At least once a week, try to do what you would do if you had millions of dollars to spare. If it doesn't make you happy, then think of a different dream.

Circle of Life…

Don't be afraid of failures, or rejections.
Keep going you'll eventually find the right way
to do and get what you want.

Circle of Life…

If you have an idea, don't let the thought of "oh, that's been done before!" stop you in your track; for "one way" doesn't always work for everyone. Surprise yourself.

Circle of Life…

Don't freak out if you outgrow your dreams. Just create a new dream.

Change is inevitable in this life, so go with the flow.

Circle of Life...

"Stand at the door of your mind and feed it something good. Read, listen, just something to feed your mind. Find a mission bigger than yourself, find a role model, secret to living is giving."

-Anthony Robbins

Circle of Life...

When you live a life of excellence and integrity, being your best, helping others, those are seeds you're sowing that will not only make your life fuller and more rewarding, but your children and grandchildren will be better because of the way you lived.

-Joel Osteen

Circle of Life…

Find yourself! Lose yourself again, it's ok.

You don't always have to have it together all the time, no one does. That's how the best lessons and treasures in life are discovered.

Circle of Life…

You can steer yourself any direction you choose.

-Dr. Seuss

Circle of Life…

You have excellence on the inside. It's who you are. It's who you were born to be.

Check out my blog at:

www.mysomewhereovertherainbow.com